ON MUSINGS
about
REAL ESTATE BUSINESS

KAREN VERSACE

© 2024 Karen Versace

All rights reserved. No part of this publication may be reproduced, distributed, or transmitted in any form or by any means, including photocopying, recording, or other electronic or mechanical methods, without the prior written permission of the publisher, except in the case of brief quotations embodied in critical reviews and certain other non-commercial uses permitted by copyright law.

ISBN: 979-8-35094-981-0

ABSTRACT

"On Musings About Real Estate Business" lays the groundwork with a focus on basic strategies. From establishing a strong online presence to mastering the art of negotiation. While the allure of part-time real estate work may seem enticing, my goal is to somehow shed some light on why it might not be the best choice. Highlighting the challenges and limitations of part-time engagement, this book provides valuable insights for those weighing their options.

This book also embarks on the basics of buying and selling a property, offering a step-by-step guide for both newbies and seasoned professionals.

Beyond the glamour of closing deals, the preparations behind-the-scenes are far more important. These legwork involved in a real estate agent's daily life. From paperwork to property inspections, this chapter underscores the multifaceted nature of the job and the importance of attention to detail.

A key aspect of any successful real estate transaction is a thorough home inspection. Chapter 5 explores the benefits of investing in quality inspections..

"On Musings About Real Estate Business" is not just a pondering of random thoughts; it's a guide to success based on experience and proven track record of the author. Packed with practical advice, real-life examples, and expert insights, this book is a must-read for anyone looking to make a mark in the industry.

*"To Agatha, Antonino, Mom, Sister, Brother, Tom, and Bailey.
This journey is dedicated to you.
Your love has built me as a realtor"*

PREFACE

WELCOME TO THE WORLD OF real estate selling, where every property tells a story and every sale marks a new chapter in someone's life. As a realtor, you are not just a salesperson; you are a storyteller, a matchmaker, and a problem solver. In this book, we will delve into the art and science of real estate selling, uncovering the techniques and secrets that will help you excel in this dynamic and competitive field.

To succeed in real estate selling, it is essential to understand the market you are operating in. The real estate market is influenced by various factors, including economic conditions, consumer preferences, and local regulations. By staying informed about current market trends and analyzing data, you can gain valuable insights that will guide your selling strategies.

First impressions matter, especially in real estate. A well-presented property not only attracts more buyers but also commands a higher price. In this section, we will discuss the importance of staging and presentation, as well as practical tips for enhancing your property's appeal. Marketing is key to selling real estate. In today's digital age, there are more marketing channels available than ever before. From social media to online listings, we will explore the various marketing strategies that can help you reach your target audience and generate leads.

Pricing a property correctly is crucial for a successful sale. Overpricing can deter potential buyers, while underpricing can result in lost revenue. We will discuss the factors that influence pricing decisions and strategies for determining the optimal price for your property.

Negotiation is an art that every realtor must master. Whether you are negotiating with buyers, sellers, or other real estate professionals, effective negotiation skills can make all the difference. We will share proven techniques for negotiating favorable deals and overcoming common obstacles. Real estate selling is governed by a complex set of laws and regulations. It is important to stay compliant with these laws to protect yourself and your clients. We will discuss key legal and ethical considerations that every realtor should be aware of.

Building strong relationships with your clients is essential for long-term success in real estate selling. We will explore strategies for building rapport, providing exceptional customer service, and maintaining client relationships even after the sale is completed.

Closing a real estate deal is often the most challenging part of the selling process. We will provide guidance on managing the closing process, handling last-minute issues, and ensuring a smooth and successful transaction. Restate selling is both an art and a science. By mastering the techniques and secrets outlined in this book, you can elevate your selling skills and achieve greater success in the competitive world of real estate.

CONTENTS

ABSTRACT
V

PREFACE
1

CHAPTER 1:
Basic Strategies for Real Estate Agents
5

CHAPTER 2:
Part-Time Real Estate: Not The Best Choice
17

CHAPTER 3:
Basics of Buying & Selling a Property
29

CHAPTER 4:
It's a Lot of Leg Work! Other Tasks of A Real Estate Agent.
39

CHAPTER 5:
The Benefits of a Good Home Inspection
51

REFERENCES AND BIBLIOGRAPHY
65

ABOUT THE AUTHOR
67

CHAPTER 1:

BASIC STRATEGIES FOR
REAL ESTATE AGENTS

In the world of real estate, success is not merely about closing deals; it's about mastering the art of client engagement, market understanding, and strategic marketing. Real estate agents today must be agile, well-informed, and innovative to thrive in an ever-evolving market landscape.

Within this chapter lies insights and strategies designed to elevate the careers of real estate agents from average to exceptional. Drawing on years of industry experience and a deep understanding of market trends, each point provides actionable insights and practical advice for agents looking to excel in their profession.

The real estate sector is currently experiencing a profound transformation, largely propelled by the rapid advancement of technology, shifts in consumer preferences, and fluctuations in economic conditions. In order to adeptly navigate this evolving landscape, real estate agents must be willing to embrace a host of new tools, adopt innovative techniques, and cultivate a mindset that is finely attuned to the prevailing market dynamics. This entails not only keeping abreast of the latest technological innovations but also understanding the changing needs and expectations of consumers in order to tailor their approach accordingly. By embracing these changes and adapting their strategies, agents can position themselves for success in this dynamic and ever-changing industry.

Establishing a strong foundation in client education and communication is paramount for real estate agents. It involves striking a delicate balance between imparting valuable knowledge to clients and building trust through effective communication. Agents must not only educate their clients about the intricacies of the real estate process but also provide them with valuable insights that can help them make informed decisions. This requires a deep understanding of the market and the ability to convey complex information in a clear and concise manner. By establishing open and honest communication channels with their clients, agents can build trust and credibility, which are essential for long-term success in the real estate industry.

In today's digital age, social media and video marketing have become indispensable tools for real estate agents. These platforms offer agents the opportunity to expand their reach, engage with clients on a more personal level, and establish a strong online presence. By leveraging the power of social media and video content, agents can showcase their listings, share valuable insights, and connect with potential clients in a more meaningful way. This not only helps agents attract new clients but also strengthens their brand and credibility in the eyes of their audience. By staying active on social media and consistently producing high-quality video content, agents can position themselves as industry leaders and stay ahead of the competition.

The real estate industry is constantly evolving, and agents must commit to ongoing learning and skill development to stay ahead. This involves staying abreast of market trends, attending relevant training programs, and honing essential skills such as negotiation and market analysis. By continuously updating their knowledge and skills, agents can better serve their clients and adapt to the ever-changing market conditions. This not only enhances their credibility as professionals but also allows them to provide their clients with the highest level of service possible. By making a commitment to continuous learning and skill development, agents can ensure their long-term success in the real estate industry.

Each chapter offers practical tips, real-life examples, and actionable strategies that agents can implement immediately to enhance their performance and achieve their professional goals. Whether you're a seasoned agent looking to stay ahead of the curve or a newcomer seeking guidance on building a successful career, this chapter provides the tools and insights you need to thrive in today's competitive real estate market.

Join us on a journey of discovery and growth as we uncover the essential strategies that will not only help you sell more but also build lasting relationships with clients, establish your brand as a trusted authority, and ultimately, take your real estate career to new heights.

Strategy 1: Establishing a Strong Foundation in Client Education and Communication

ESTABLISHING A STRONG FOUNDATION IN client education and communication is crucial for real estate agents. It's about more than just providing information; it's about empowering clients with the knowledge they need to make informed decisions. Effective communication is the key to building trust, fostering relationships, and creating a sense of partnership between agent and client.

Understanding client needs. To excel in client education and communication, agents must first understand the needs and preferences of their clients. This requires active listening, empathy, and the ability to tailor communication styles to suit individual clients. By taking the time to understand clients' goals and concerns, agents can provide them with the information they need in a way that is meaningful and relevant to them.

Tailoring communication styles. One key aspect of understanding client needs is recognizing that each client is unique. What works for one client may not work for another. Agents must be adaptable and willing to adjust their approach to communication based on the individual client's preferences. This may involve using different communication channels, such as phone calls, emails, or in-person meetings, depending on what the client is most comfortable with.

Providing market insights. In addition to educating clients about the real estate process, agents must also provide them with insights into the market. This includes understanding market trends, pricing dynamics, and the local economy. By keeping clients informed about market conditions, agents can help them make strategic decisions about buying or selling property.

Explaining market concepts: Agents should also be prepared to answer questions and provide explanations about market concepts that may be unfamiliar to clients. This may include explaining terms such as "comparative market analysis" or "days on market," and helping clients understand how these factors can impact their buying or selling decisions.

Building trust is key to effective communication: Clients need to feel confident that their agent has their best interests at heart and is working diligently on their behalf. This requires transparency, honesty, and integrity in all interactions. By consistently demonstrating these qualities, agents can build strong, lasting relationships with their clients.

Being proactive in addressing issues is one way to build trust is by being proactive in addressing issues or concerns that arise during a real estate transaction. This may involve keeping clients informed about potential challenges, such as inspection issues or financing delays, and offering solutions to mitigate these issues. By being transparent about the process and responsive to client needs, agents can build trust and credibility with their clients.

Handling challenges with grace. Open and honest communication is crucial when dealing with challenges or obstacles in a real estate transaction. Agents must be proactive in addressing issues, providing timely updates, and offering solutions. By keeping clients informed and involved throughout the process, agents can mitigate stress and build trust.

Remaining calm and composed. It's important for agents to remain calm and composed in challenging situations, and to approach problems with a solutions-oriented mindset. This may involve brainstorming creative solutions, seeking advice from colleagues or mentors, and working collaboratively with clients to find the best way forward.

Strategy 2: Social Media and Video Marketing

In today's digital age, social media and video marketing have become indispensable tools for real estate agents. These platforms offer agents the opportunity to expand their reach, engage with clients on a more personal level, and establish a strong online presence. By leveraging the power of social media and video content, agents can showcase their listings, share valuable insights, and connect with potential clients in a more meaningful way. This not only helps agents attract new clients but also strengthens their brand and credibility in the eyes of their audience. By staying active on social media and consistently producing high-quality video content, agents can position themselves as industry leaders and stay ahead of the competition.

Social Media Marketing platforms such as Facebook, Instagram, and Twitter allow agents to reach a wide audience of potential clients with targeted marketing messages. These platforms have user-friendly interfaces that make it easy for agents to create posts, share photos and videos, and engage with their audience.

Facebook, with its vast user base, is an ideal platform for real estate agents to showcase their listings. Agents can create business pages, post photos and videos of properties, and use targeted advertising to reach potential buyers. Facebook also offers features like live video, which allows agents to give virtual tours of properties and engage with viewers in real-time.

Instagram is another powerful platform for real estate marketing, particularly for visually appealing properties. Agents can use Instagram to share high-quality photos and videos of their listings, as well as behind-the-scenes glimpses of their work. Instagram's Stories feature is especially useful for creating ephemeral content that generates excitement and urgency among followers.

Twitter is a great platform for real-time updates and engagement. Agents can use Twitter to share market insights, industry news, and updates on new listings. Twitter's use of hashtags makes it easy for agents to reach a wider audience and join relevant conversations in the real estate industry.

Video marketing has become increasingly popular in the real estate industry, as it allows agents to create engaging and informative content that can be easily shared and viewed by a large audience. Videos are more likely to grab the attention of potential clients than text-based content, making them an effective tool for showcasing properties and building brand awareness.

Agents can create various types of videos to market their listings and establish themselves as industry experts. Property tour videos allow agents to give viewers a virtual tour of a property, highlighting its key features and amenities. These videos can be posted on social media platforms, shared on websites, and sent to clients via email.

Another type of video that agents can create is the "meet the agent" video, which introduces them to potential clients and gives them a glimpse into their personality and expertise. These videos help to humanize the agent and build trust with clients.

Agents can also create videos that provide valuable tips and advice for home buyers and sellers. These videos demonstrate the agent's knowledge and expertise, positioning them as a helpful resource for clients.

Social media and video marketing are powerful tools that real estate agents can use to expand their reach, engage with clients, and establish themselves as industry leaders. By leveraging these platforms effectively, agents can attract more clients, showcase their listings, and build a strong online presence that sets them apart from the competition.

Strategy 3: Continuous Learning and Skill Development

In the dynamic world of real estate, adaptability and expertise are the keys to success. Embracing a mindset of continuous learning and skill development is not just an option; it's a necessity for thriving in this competitive industry. Here's how agents can effectively implement this strategy:

Market Trends Analysis: The real estate market is in a constant state of flux, influenced by various factors such as economic indicators, government policies, and societal trends. Agents must stay informed about these changes to anticipate market movements and advise their clients accordingly. Regularly analyzing market trends through reputable sources and industry reports is crucial.

Training Programs and Courses: Attending training programs and courses tailored to the real estate industry is essential for staying updated with the latest practices and techniques. These programs often cover topics such as legal updates, technology tools, and best practices in client service. Agents should actively seek out these opportunities to enhance their skills and knowledge base.

Skill Refinement: Negotiation, communication, and market analysis are core skills that every real estate agent should continually refine. Negotiation skills, for example, can be honed through practice, role-playing scenarios, and seeking feedback from experienced professionals. Effective communication, both verbal and written, is critical for building rapport with clients and closing deals.

Networking and Collaboration: Learning from peers and industry experts is invaluable. Networking events, conferences, and online forums provide opportunities to exchange ideas, share experiences, and gain insights into emerging trends. Collaborating with other professionals, such as mortgage brokers, home inspectors, and contractors, can also broaden an agent's knowledge base and skill set.

Professional Certifications: Obtaining relevant professional certifications demonstrates a commitment to excellence and can enhance an agent's credibility. Certifications such as the Certified Residential Specialist (CRS) or the Accredited Buyer's Representative (ABR) designation signify expertise in specific areas of real estate, boosting client confidence.

Technology Adoption: Embracing technology is essential for staying competitive in the modern real estate landscape. Agents should familiarize themselves with the latest real estate software, marketing tools, and digital platforms to streamline their processes and reach a wider audience.

Mentorship and Coaching: Seeking mentorship from seasoned professionals or hiring a real estate coach can provide personalized guidance and accelerate learning. Mentors can offer valuable insights, help navigate challenges, and provide encouragement along the way.

Feedback and Evaluation: Regularly seeking feedback from clients, colleagues, and supervisors is crucial for identifying areas for improvement. Conducting self-evaluations and setting professional development goals can help agents track their progress and stay motivated.

By embracing a culture of continuous learning and skill development, real estate agents can adapt to market dynamics, enhance their professional competence, and ultimately, achieve long-term success in the industry.

Strategy 4: Networking

BUILDING A STRONG NETWORK OF professionals in related industries is a powerful strategy for real estate agents to enhance their service offerings and provide added value to their clients. Networking allows agents to connect with mortgage brokers, contractors, home inspectors, and other professionals, creating a collaborative environment that benefits everyone involved. Here's how agents can effectively build and leverage their network:

1. **Identifying Key Contacts:** The first step in building a strong network is identifying key contacts in related industries. These may include mortgage brokers who can help clients secure financing, contractors who can assist with home renovations, and home inspectors who can provide thorough property assessments. Agents should also consider connecting with professionals in complementary industries, such as interior designers or landscapers, to offer comprehensive services to their clients.

2. **Attend Networking Events:** Networking events, such as industry conferences, trade shows, and local meetups, provide valuable opportunities to connect with other professionals. Agents should actively participate in these events, engage in conversations, and exchange contact information with potential collaborators. These events can also provide insights into industry trends and best practices.

3. **Utilize Online Platforms:** Online networking platforms, such as LinkedIn and real estate forums, are valuable tools for expanding one's professional network. Agents can join industry-specific groups, participate in discussions, and connect with professionals from around the world. These platforms also provide a platform for showcasing expertise and building credibility within the industry.

4. **Offer Value to Your Network:** Building a strong network is not just about making connections; it's also about offering value to your contacts. Agents can share relevant industry insights, refer clients to other professionals in their network, and collaborate on marketing initiatives. By providing value to their network, agents can strengthen relationships and foster a sense of reciprocity.

5. **Maintain Regular Contact:** Networking is an ongoing process that requires regular communication and engagement. Agents should make an effort to stay in touch with their network, whether through email, phone calls, or in-person meetings. Keeping lines of communication open ensures that agents remain top-of-mind when opportunities for collaboration arise.

6. **Attend Industry Seminars and Workshops:** Industry seminars and workshops provide a wealth of knowledge and networking opportunities. Agents can learn about the latest industry trends, expand their skill set, and connect with other professionals in a learning environment. These events can also lead to new business opportunities and collaborations.

7. **Follow Up:** After making initial connections, it's important to follow up with new contacts to solidify the relationship. Agents can send a follow-up email or message, connect on social media, or schedule a follow-up meeting to discuss potential collaboration opportunities further.

By actively building and maintaining a strong network of professionals in related industries, real estate agents can enhance their service offerings, provide added value to their clients, and position themselves as trusted advisors in the industry. Networking is a powerful tool that can open doors to new opportunities and lead to long-term success in the real estate business.

CHAPTER 2:

PART-TIME REAL ESTATE: NOT THE BEST CHOICE

The prospect of part-time work often holds a certain charm. The flexibility it offers, the opportunity to test the waters without fully immersing oneself, and the potential to supplement other commitments can all be attractive propositions. However, it's essential to delve deeper into this seemingly appealing option before embarking on a part-time real estate journey.

The real estate industry is a complex and demanding field that requires a significant investment of time and effort. It's not just about showing properties and closing deals. It involves market research, networking, marketing, negotiation, and a deep understanding of legal and financial aspects. These responsibilities can be overwhelming for part-time agents who may struggle to dedicate the necessary time and energy.

Flexibility, while an advantage, can also be a double-edged sword. The ability to work at one's own pace and choose one's hours can lead to complacency. Real estate is a highly competitive field, and success often depends on being available and responsive. Clients may require assistance at odd hours, and deals can come up unexpectedly. Part-time agents may find it challenging to keep up with these demands and may lose out on opportunities to those who are fully committed to the industry.

Moreover, building a reputation and a strong network is crucial in real estate. This requires consistent effort, participation in industry events, and staying updated with market trends. Part-time agents may find it difficult to establish their presence in the industry and gain the trust of clients and other professionals. They may also struggle to stay abreast of the ever-changing market dynamics, legal regulations, and technological advancements.

Financial stability is another aspect to consider. Real estate income is often commission-based, and it can be unpredictable. It may take time to close the first deal, and dry spells are not uncommon. For those relying on real estate as a supplementary income, this unpredictability can cause financial stress.

Lastly, the emotional toll should not be underestimated. The highs and lows, the stress of negotiations, the disappointment of lost deals, and the pressure to meet clients' expectations can be emotionally draining. Balancing these pressures with other commitments can be challenging for part-time agents.

While part-time work in real estate may seem appealing, it comes with its own set of challenges. It requires a high level of commitment, resilience, and dedication that goes beyond the allure of flexibility and supplementary income. Therefore, it's crucial to thoroughly understand these challenges before deciding to embark on a part-time real estate journey. In many cases, a full-time commitment to the profession may be a wiser choice. It allows for a deeper understanding of the industry, more opportunities for growth, and a greater chance of success. However, if one chooses the part-time path, going in with clear expectations and a solid plan can help navigate the challenges and make the most of the opportunities.

1. Competing Against Full-Time Professionals

IMAGINE STEPPING ONTO A RACETRACK where your competitors have been training relentlessly, day in and day out, while you can only dedicate a fraction of that time. This analogy holds true in the real estate world. Full-time agents live and breathe the market, constantly honing their skills, and networking. To compete with them on a part-time basis is an uphill battle that few can win.

In the world of real estate, full-time professionals have the advantage of time. They spend their days immersed in the industry, studying market trends, visiting properties, meeting with clients, and negotiating deals. Their workday is dedicated to understanding the ins and outs of the market, and they have the time to react quickly to new listings or changes in the market.

On the other hand, part-time real estate agents often juggle their real estate duties with other commitments, such as a full-time job or family responsibilities. This means they have less time to dedicate to studying the market, visiting properties, and meeting with clients. They may not be able to respond as quickly to new listings or changes in the market, which can put them at a disadvantage.

Furthermore, full-time agents often have a larger network of contacts in the industry. They may have relationships with other agents, lenders, and service providers, which can be beneficial when negotiating deals or solving problems for their clients. Part-time agents, on the other hand, may not have as extensive a network, which can limit their ability to provide the best service to their clients.

However, this doesn't mean that part-time agents can't be successful. It simply means they need to be strategic about how they use their time and resources. They may need to focus on a specific niche or geographic area where they can leverage their knowledge and skills. They may also need to invest in tools and technology that can help them stay connected and responsive, even when they're not working full-time.

In conclusion, while competing against full-time professionals in the real estate industry can be challenging, it's not impossible. With the right strategy and resources, part-time agents can carve out a successful career in the industry. But they need to be aware of the challenges and be prepared to put in the work to overcome them. After all, in the race of real estate, it's not just about who runs the fastest, but who runs the smartest.

2. The Snowball Effect of Full-Time Commitment

In the realm of real estate, the concept of full-time commitment is not merely a choice; it is a strategic decision that can significantly influence one's trajectory towards success. This commitment, akin to a snowball rolling down a hill, gathers momentum with each interaction and deal closed, thereby creating a powerful effect of productivity and income.

The real estate industry is a dynamic and interactive field. It thrives on relationships, networking, and constant engagement with various stakeholders, including buyers, sellers, investors, and other real estate professionals. Each interaction presents an opportunity - a potential lead, a referral, or valuable market insight. The more active a real estate professional is, the more they expose themselves to these opportunities.

Every deal closed is not just a transaction; it is a testament to the real estate professional's skills, knowledge, and dedication. It enhances their reputation, expands their network, and often leads to referrals. Each successful deal adds to the professional's momentum, much like a snowball growing larger and faster as it rolls down a hill. This snowball effect is not merely about increasing size or speed; it's about enhancing impact. A larger, faster snowball has a greater impact when it reaches its destination. Similarly, a real estate professional with a robust portfolio of successful deals and a wide network can command better deals, attract quality leads, and negotiate more effectively.

However, this snowball effect is significantly slowed down in the case of part-time work. Part-time commitment in real estate can limit the number of interactions and potential deals, slowing down the momentum. It can make it harder for the professional to stay updated with market trends, maintain relationships, and respond promptly to opportunities. This can lead to slower progression and lesser returns. Moreover, full-time commitment in real estate is a signal to clients and other professionals about the individual's seriousness and dedication to the field. It builds trust and credibility, which are crucial in the real estate business.

Full-time commitment in real estate sets off a snowball effect of productivity and income. It allows professionals to fully immerse themselves in the industry, seize opportunities, close more deals, and ultimately, achieve greater success. While part-time work may suit some individuals, it is the full-time commitment that truly harnesses the snowball effect, propelling real estate professionals towards significant returns and success.

3. The Speed of the Real Estate Market

Real estate is a dynamic field, characterized by its constant ebb and flow. Every day brings new listings, sales, and changes in property status. This fast-paced environment is a reflection of the various factors that influence the real estate market, including economic conditions, interest rates, and consumer confidence.

Staying on top of this fast-paced environment is critical for any real estate professional. Clients expect you to have up-to-the-minute information on properties, pricing, and market trends. They rely on your expertise and knowledge to guide them through the complexities of buying or selling a property.

Doing this part-time makes it challenging to keep pace with the market. The real estate market doesn't pause or slow down for anyone. Properties can be listed and sold within a matter of days, and prices can fluctuate based on supply and demand. If you're not fully committed to monitoring these changes, you could potentially miss out on opportunities, costing you deals. The speed of the real estate market also impacts how you interact with clients. In a fast-paced market, you need to be able to quickly provide clients with accurate, relevant information. This requires a deep understanding of the market and a commitment to staying informed about the latest trends and developments.

In addition, the speed of the real estate market can affect your marketing strategies. In a slow market, you might have more time to showcase a property and attract potential buyers. But in a fast-paced market, you need to be able to quickly generate interest and facilitate sales.

Overall, the speed of the real estate market is a crucial aspect of the industry. It influences everything from the way you interact with clients to the strategies you use to market properties. Staying on top of this fast-paced environment is key to your success as a real estate professional.

Remember, the real estate market waits for no one. It's a dynamic, fast-paced industry that requires dedication, knowledge, and a keen eye for trends. Whether you're working part-time or full-time, staying abreast of the market's speed is crucial. It could mean the difference between closing a deal or losing one. So, keep your finger on the pulse of the market, and you'll be well-equipped to navigate its speed and volatility.

4. The Need for a Flexible Schedule

IN THE DYNAMIC WORLD OF real estate, the concept of a traditional 9-to-5 work schedule is virtually non-existent. The industry thrives on the principle of availability and adaptability, making a flexible schedule not just an advantage, but a necessity for success.

One of the defining characteristics of successful real estate agents is their ability to be available when their clients need them. This is because clients, much like the properties they seek, come with their own unique set of requirements and schedules. Some may prefer early morning meetings before their day begins, while others may only be available for late-night discussions after their workday ends. Weekend property viewings, holiday negotiations, and last-minute showings are all part and parcel of a real estate agent's job.

The unpredictable nature of the real estate market further underscores the need for flexibility. Market trends can shift rapidly, and new properties can come up for sale with little to no notice. Being able to swiftly respond to these changes can mean the difference between closing a deal and losing one. Moreover, real estate transactions are often time-sensitive. Delays in communication or unavailability can lead to missed opportunities, and in a competitive market, this can be detrimental to your business. A part-time commitment or rigid schedule often means missing out on these opportunities.

However, it's important to note that having a flexible schedule doesn't mean being available 24/7. It's about smart time management and setting clear expectations with clients. Successful agents know how to balance their personal life with their professional commitments, ensuring they're able to provide the best service to their clients without burning out.

A flexible schedule is more than just a convenience in the real estate business - it's a critical factor in building a successful career. It allows agents to meet the diverse needs of their clients, respond quickly to market changes, and seize opportunities as they arise. As the real estate landscape continues to evolve, the agents who can adapt their schedules and routines to meet these changes are the ones who will thrive.

5. Building Relationships and Credibility

RELATIONSHIPS ARE THE CORNERSTONE OF success. The real estate industry is as much about fostering connections as it is about transactions. The ability to build trust and rapport with clients and other agents is not just a desirable trait, but an essential one. It is a complex web of interactions, negotiations, and transactions. It's a field where the human element is as crucial as the financial one. The relationships you build can make or break your career. They can open doors to new opportunities, or they can close them.

Part-time agents often face a unique set of challenges in establishing themselves in the industry. Their commitment level may be questioned by others, leading to skepticism and doubt. This can result in missed opportunities and a slower path to success.

However, it's important to note that being a part-time agent doesn't necessarily equate to a lack of commitment or ability. Many part-time agents are highly dedicated and capable professionals. They bring a unique perspective and can offer flexible availability that full-time agents may not be able to provide. The key to overcoming these challenges lies in demonstrating credibility and building strong relationships. This involves showing clients and other agents that you are reliable, knowledgeable, and committed to your work. It means going the extra mile to provide excellent service and to meet the needs of your clients.

Building relationships in real estate also extends beyond your clients. It involves networking with other agents, brokers, and professionals in the industry. These relationships can provide valuable opportunities for collaboration and mutual growth. They can also offer a source of support and advice, helping you navigate the challenges of the industry.

Credibility, on the other hand, is earned through consistent performance and professional conduct. It's about proving your worth through actions, not just words. This means staying updated with the latest market trends, being honest and transparent in your dealings, and always putting the best interests of your clients first. Building relationships and credibility in real estate is not a one-time effort. It's a continuous process that requires patience, persistence, and genuine care for the people you work with. It's about showing up, day after day, ready to serve your clients and contribute to the industry.

Remember, in real estate, your reputation is your most valuable asset. It's what sets you apart in a competitive market. It's what attracts clients to you and keeps them coming back. So, invest time and effort in building strong relationships and establishing your credibility. It will pay off in the long run, leading to a successful and fulfilling career in real estate. The path may be challenging, especially for part-time agents. But with determination, professionalism, and a focus on building relationships and credibility, success is not just a possibility, but an achievable reality.

When does a part-time in real estate business work?

THE WORLD OF REAL ESTATE is a vast and diverse landscape, filled with opportunities for those who dare to venture into it. While it is often perceived as a full-time endeavor, there are instances where part-time engagement in real estate can be a viable and even advantageous option.

The challenges of part-time real estate are undeniable. Balancing a regular job with the demands of real estate can be daunting. The unpredictable nature of the market, the need for constant networking, and the time-consuming process of closing deals are just a few of the hurdles that part-time real estate agents face. However, these challenges should not deter one from considering part-time real estate as a feasible option.

One of the key factors that make part-time real estate work is having a flexible schedule. If your primary job allows for unconventional hours, such as working nights or weekends, you may find that you can dedicate enough time to real estate to be successful. This flexibility allows you to attend to your clients' needs, conduct property viewings, and negotiate deals at times that are convenient for your clients, thereby increasing your chances of success.

Another factor that makes part-time real estate a viable option is the opportunity to test the waters before diving in. Real estate is a significant commitment, both in terms of time and financial investment. If you're unsure about making this commitment, starting part-time can be a prudent choice. It allows you to gain firsthand experience of the industry without the pressure of relying on it for your primary income. This way, you can assess whether you have the passion, skills, and resilience required to thrive in the real estate industry.

Moreover, part-time real estate can serve as a stepping stone to a full-time career in the industry. As you gain experience, build your network, and establish your reputation, you may find that real estate is indeed your calling. Transitioning from part-time to full-time then becomes a natural progression, made easier by the foundation you've built during your part-time stint.

Part-time real estate also offers the advantage of financial security. With a regular job providing a steady income, you can navigate the volatile real estate market with less financial stress. This security can empower you to take calculated risks, such as investing in properties or taking on challenging clients, which could potentially lead to higher returns.

In essence, part-time real estate is not merely a compromise but can be a strategic choice, depending on one's circumstances and goals. It offers a unique blend of flexibility, security, and opportunity that can pave the way for success in the real estate industry. While it may not be the conventional route, it is certainly a path worth considering for those who wish to explore the world of real estate at their own pace and on their own terms. As with any endeavor, success in part-time real estate ultimately depends on one's dedication, adaptability, and perseverance. With these qualities, part-time real estate can indeed work.

While the allure of part-time real estate may seem enticing, it's essential to understand the challenges and limitations it presents. Competing with full-time professionals, keeping up with the market, maintaining a flexible schedule, and building relationships are all crucial aspects that can be hindered by a part-time commitment. Consider your circumstances carefully before embarking on a part-time real estate journey, and ensure you can dedicate the time and effort necessary for success.

CHAPTER 3:

BASICS OF BUYING & SELLING A PROPERTY

IN THIS CHAPTER, WE WILL tackle the core principles of buying and selling properties in the real estate market. Picture yourself as a homeowner, ready to part ways with your property. You've made the decision to engage the services of a real estate sales representative to guide you through this intricate process.

The first section of this chapter will focus on understanding the real estate market. We will dissect the factors that influence the market, such as economic conditions, interest rates, and demographic trends. We will also delve into the importance of location and timing in real estate transactions.

Next, we will turn our attention to the role of the real estate sales representative. We will discuss how they can provide valuable insights into the market, assist in setting a competitive price for your property, and effectively market it to potential buyers. We will also touch on the legal and ethical responsibilities of a sales representative.

Following this, we will explore the process of preparing your property for sale. This includes understanding the importance of first impressions, staging your home to attract buyers, and making necessary repairs or upgrades. We will also discuss the role of home inspections and appraisals in the selling process.

In the subsequent section, we will delve into the negotiation process. We will discuss how to handle offers and counteroffers, the importance of negotiation strategies, and how to navigate through the closing process. We will also touch on potential challenges that may arise during negotiations and how to overcome them.

Finally, we will discuss the post-sale process. This includes understanding the legal documents involved, the process of transferring ownership, and the costs associated with selling a property. We will also provide tips on how to handle the emotional aspect of selling your home.

Throughout this chapter, we will provide practical examples and tips to help you navigate the complex world of real estate transactions. Our aim is to equip you with the knowledge and confidence to successfully sell your property.

As we journey through this chapter, remember that selling a property is not just a financial decision, but also an emotional one. It's about closing one chapter of your life and starting a new one. So, let's embark on this journey together, exploring the fascinating world of real estate transactions.

Seller Representation

When you decide to sell your property, one of the first steps you'll take is to contact a real estate sales representative. This professional will guide you through the complex process of selling your home, from listing it on the market to closing the deal.

The relationship between you and your real estate sales representative is formalized through a contract known as a listing agreement. This agreement outlines the responsibilities of both parties and sets the commission fee that the representative will earn upon the successful sale of your property. For the purpose of this discussion, we'll assume a commission fee of five percent based on the purchase price. This percentage can vary depending on the market conditions and the negotiation between the seller and the representative.

Once the listing agreement is signed, the real estate sales representative will create a Multiple Listing Service (MLS) sheet. The MLS is a database used by real estate professionals to list properties for sale. The MLS sheet for your property will contain crucial information that potential buyers will want to know. This includes the asking price, the number of bedrooms and bathrooms, the size of the property, the type of property (e.g., single-family home, condo, townhouse), and any unique features or amenities.

The MLS sheet also specifies the cooperating brokerage commission. This is the portion of the commission fee that will be paid to any other real estate sales representative who brings a buyer for your property. By offering a cooperating brokerage commission, you incentivize other representatives to show your property to their clients, increasing the visibility of your listing and the likelihood of a quick sale.

The real estate sales representative will then market your property to potential buyers. This can involve a variety of strategies, including online listings, open houses, private showings, and direct mail campaigns. Throughout this process, the representative will communicate with you regularly to provide updates and feedback from showings.

Once a buyer makes an offer on your property, the real estate sales representative will help you negotiate the terms of the sale. They will ensure that you understand all the terms of the contract and that your interests are protected. After the contract is signed, the representative will coordinate the closing process, which includes handling paperwork, arranging for inspections and appraisals, and ensuring that the buyer secures financing.

Selling a property is a complex process that involves numerous steps and a significant amount of paperwork. By working with a real estate sales representative, you can navigate this process with confidence, knowing that a professional is guiding you every step of the way. Their expertise and knowledge of the real estate market can help you sell your property quickly and for the best possible price.

Buyer Representation

IN THE REALM OF REAL estate, the process of buying and selling properties is not a solitary endeavor. It involves a network of professionals, each with their specific roles and responsibilities. One of these key players is the buyer's sales representative. This individual plays a crucial role in the transaction, acting as the liaison between the buyer and the seller, and ensuring that the buyer's interests are well-represented.

After some time on the market, you find a buyer who is represented by another sales representative. This is a common scenario in real estate transactions. The buyer's sales representative is tasked with guiding the buyer through the process, providing advice and assistance, and ultimately helping the buyer secure the property they desire. The buyer's sales representative also has a commission agreement. In this example, we'll say it's 2.5 percent of the purchase price. This commission serves as the representative's compensation for their services. It's a standard practice in the industry and is usually factored into the financial considerations of the transaction.

The buyer presents an offer, matching your asking price of $100,000. This is an ideal situation for a seller. It means that the property was priced correctly and that the buyer sees the value in the asking price. The offer comes with no conditions, which simplifies the transaction and reduces potential obstacles to the sale. The closing date is set for one month from the offer date. This is a typical timeframe for real estate transactions, allowing ample time for all parties to fulfill their respective obligations. It provides the buyer time to finalize their financing, and the seller time to prepare for the move.

Additionally, the buyer provides a $5,000 security deposit. This is a good faith deposit, demonstrating the buyer's serious intent to purchase the property. It provides the seller with some level of assurance that the buyer is committed to the transaction. In this scenario, the buyer's sales representative has effectively facilitated a smooth transaction. They have negotiated a deal that satisfies their client's needs and aligns with the seller's expectations. This is the essence of buyer representation - ensuring that the buyer's interests are protected, while also fostering a fair and successful transaction for all parties involved.

As we delve deeper into the intricacies of real estate transactions, it becomes increasingly clear that buyer representation is not just about finding a property and making an offer. It's about understanding the market, negotiating effectively, navigating the legalities of the transaction, and ultimately, ensuring that the buyer's journey to property ownership is as smooth and successful as possible. This is the value that a competent and dedicated buyer's sales representative brings to the table. And it's why their role is so integral in the world of real estate.

In the end, the success of a real estate transaction is often a testament to the skills and expertise of the buyer's sales representative. Their ability to represent their client's interests, negotiate effectively, and navigate the complexities of the transaction is invaluable. It's a role that requires a deep understanding of the market, strong negotiation skills, and a commitment to client service. And when done right, it can make all the difference in a successful real estate transaction.

Closing the Deal

THE PROCESS OF CLOSING A real estate deal is a critical juncture in the property transaction process. It is the point where ownership of the property is transferred from the seller to the buyer. This process begins once both parties agree to the offer. The agreement signifies a mutual understanding between the buyer and the seller about the terms and conditions of the sale.

The first step in closing the deal involves the buyer handing over the deposit. This deposit, often referred to as earnest money, is placed in a trust account. It serves as a sign of the buyer's serious intent to purchase the property and is typically held by a neutral third party, such as a real estate brokerage or a lawyer.

Following the placement of the deposit, the lawyers representing the buyer and seller take over. These legal representatives play a crucial role in ensuring that all legal requirements are met leading up to the closing date. They review the purchase agreement, verify the title and deed, coordinate the payment of fees, and ensure that all necessary documents are correctly signed and delivered.

As the closing date approaches, the buyer prepares to pay the remaining balance of the purchase price. In our example, this amount is $95,000. However, the buyer must also be prepared to cover any additional closing costs. These costs may include title insurance, appraisal fees, inspection fees, escrow fees, and loan origination fees. It's essential for the buyer to be aware of these potential costs to avoid any surprises on the closing date.

On the closing date, the buyer's payment is typically made to the seller's lawyer. This lawyer acts as an intermediary, ensuring that the funds are correctly distributed and that all legal obligations are met. The payment process is carefully orchestrated to ensure that all parties involved in the transaction are protected.

Once the payment is received, the seller will then receive the agreed-upon amount of $95,000, minus any legal fees and other expenses. These deductions may include real estate agent commissions, transfer taxes, or any outstanding balances on the property's mortgage or liens. The seller's lawyer will ensure that these amounts are correctly calculated and deducted from the sale proceeds.

With the completion of these steps, the transaction is considered closed. The buyer is now the legal owner of the property, and the seller has successfully sold their property. This marks the end of the real estate transaction process, but it also signifies the beginning of the buyer's journey as a property owner.

The closing of the deal is a complex process that requires careful coordination between various parties. It involves multiple steps, each of which must be executed with precision to ensure a smooth and successful transaction. By understanding these steps, both buyers and sellers can navigate the closing process with confidence and ease.

Commission Payments

IN REAL ESTATE, COMMISSION PAYMENTS are a critical component of the transaction process. They serve as the primary source of income for the sales representatives involved in the deal. These payments are typically derived from the deposit made by the buyer.

The seller's sales representative is the first to receive their share of the commission. This payment is not without deductions, however. Brokerage fees, which are costs associated with the use of the brokerage's services and resources, are subtracted from the commission. These fees can cover a range of expenses, including administrative costs, marketing, and the use of office space or proprietary software.

Once the brokerage fees are deducted, the remaining amount is what the seller's sales representative takes home. This structure incentivizes sales representatives to secure higher selling prices, as their commission will increase correspondingly.

The cooperating brokerage, which could be seen as a partner or ally in the transaction, receives the remaining commission. This brokerage could represent another seller or a buyer. The distribution of commission to the cooperating brokerage fosters a spirit of collaboration and mutual benefit among different brokerages. It encourages them to work together to facilitate transactions, knowing that they share in the financial rewards.

On the other side of the transaction, we have the buyer's brokerage. This entity also pays out a commission to the buyer's sales representative, following a similar structure. Brokerage fees are deducted, and the remaining amount constitutes the sales representative's earnings.

This system mirrors that of the seller's side, creating symmetry in the transaction process. It ensures that all parties - the seller's sales representative, the buyer's sales representative, and their respective brokerages - are motivated to work towards the common goal of closing the deal.

The commission structure in real estate transactions is a delicate balance of incentives and rewards. It ensures that all parties involved are adequately compensated for their efforts. At the same time, it encourages cooperation and competition, driving the market towards efficiency and growth.

This intricate web of commissions and fees, while complex, is a fundamental aspect of the real estate business. It fuels the industry, propelling transactions forward and ensuring that every successful deal results in fair compensation for those who made it possible. As such, understanding this system is crucial for anyone looking to navigate the real estate market, whether as a buyer, a seller, or a sales representative.

By comprehending the mechanics of commission payments, individuals can make informed decisions and negotiate better deals, ultimately leading to more successful and profitable transactions. Thus, the knowledge of how commission payments work is not just beneficial—it's essential for success in the real estate business.

CHAPTER 4:

IT'S A LOT OF LEG WORK! OTHER TASKS OF A REAL ESTATE AGENT.

TITLE SEARCH AND INSURANCE

The process of buying a property involves numerous steps, each crucial in its own right. One such step is the title search and insurance, which plays a pivotal role in ensuring a smooth and secure transaction. A title search is an exhaustive examination of public records to confirm the legal ownership of the property and to find out if there are any claims or liens against it. This process is crucial as it helps to avoid potential legal disputes over the property's ownership. It's conducted by a title company or an attorney, who meticulously reviews court records, deeds, and other documents spanning many years.

The primary purpose of a title search is to ascertain that the person selling the property has the legal right to do so and that there are no outstanding claims or liens against it. These could include unpaid taxes, unsatisfied mortgages, judgements against the seller, and restrictions limiting the use of the land.

If a claim is discovered after the property has been purchased, it can lead to financial loss or, in a worst-case scenario, loss of the property. This is where title insurance comes into play. Title insurance is a form of indemnity insurance that protects the holder from financial loss sustained from defects in a title to a property. There are two types of title insurance: owner's title insurance, which protects the property owner, and lender's title insurance, which protects the lender.

Unlike traditional insurance policies that protect against future events, title insurance protects against claims for past occurrences. These claims could arise due to a variety of circumstances, such as fraud, forgery, undisclosed heirs, and mistakes in the public record.

The cost of title insurance can vary widely depending on the property, the state where you are buying, and the insurance provider. However, it's typically a one-time charge that's paid at closing.

While title insurance isn't mandatory, it's highly recommended. Without it, homeowners could potentially face significant financial damage or even lose their homes if a claim is made against their property. The process of title search and insurance is a vital part of the real estate transaction. It provides peace of mind to both buyers and lenders, ensuring that the property they are investing in is free from legal encumbrances and is rightfully theirs.

By understanding the importance of title search and insurance, individuals can navigate the complex world of real estate with confidence, secure in the knowledge that their investment is protected. This understanding is a crucial component of any successful real estate business. It underscores the importance of due diligence and the value of protecting one's investment against potential legal and financial pitfalls.

Remember, a well-informed buyer is a confident buyer. And in the world of real estate, confidence is key. So, whether you're a first-time homebuyer or a seasoned investor, never underestimate the importance of a thorough title search and the protection offered by title insurance. It's not just about buying a property—it's about safeguarding your investment for years to come.

ESCROW AND CLOSING COSTS

In real estate transactions, the terms "escrow" and "closing costs" are frequently encountered. They play a crucial role in ensuring a smooth, secure, and fair property transfer from the seller to the buyer.

THE ROLE OF ESCROW

The escrow process begins once both parties have agreed on a price and signed a purchase agreement. At this point, the buyer's earnest money deposit is placed into an escrow account. This account is held by a neutral third party, often a title company or an escrow firm, acting on behalf of both the buyer and seller.

The primary purpose of escrow is to protect all parties involved. The buyer can be assured that the seller will not abscond with their earnest money before the deal is finalized. Conversely, the seller has assurance that the buyer is committed to purchasing the property, as demonstrated by the earnest money deposit.

During the escrow period, several conditions must be met before the transaction can be finalized. These conditions often include home inspections, mortgage approval for the buyer, title search, and any negotiated repairs. The escrow holder ensures that these conditions are met before releasing funds and transferring the property title to the buyer.

UNDERSTANDING CLOSING COSTS

Closing costs are an assortment of fees separate from the home's purchase price. They include a variety of expenses incurred during the home buying and selling process. Some of the most common closing costs include fees for the title search, appraisal, legal services, and loan origination.

A title search is a thorough examination of public records to confirm the seller's legal ownership of the property and discover any liens, unpaid taxes, or other claims. An appraisal involves a professional assessment of the property's value to ensure that the agreed-upon sale price is appropriate.

Legal services in a real estate transaction ensure that all legal aspects, including the drafting and review of documents, are correctly handled. Loan origination fees cover the lender's costs of processing the new loan application.

DISTRIBUTION OF COSTS

Typically, both the buyer and seller have responsibilities for covering closing costs, as outlined in the purchase agreement. While practices can vary by region and individual negotiations, the buyer often covers costs related to their mortgage loan, and the seller covers the title transfer fees.

However, everything is negotiable in a real estate transaction, including closing costs. In some cases, sellers may agree to pay a portion of the closing costs to incentivize a sale or help a buyer with limited funds.

In summary, escrow and closing costs are integral parts of a real estate transaction. They provide a structured, secure framework that protects both the buyer and seller, ensuring that all conditions are met before the property changes hands. Understanding these processes can help individuals navigate the complex landscape of real estate transactions with confidence and peace of mind.

POST-CLOSING RESPONSIBILITIES

The closing of a real estate transaction signifies the end of a complex process involving numerous steps, from property viewing to price negotiation, contract signing, and finally, the transfer of ownership. However, the responsibilities of both the buyer and the seller do not end at the closing table. There are several post-closing responsibilities that both parties need to fulfill to ensure a smooth transition.

SELLER'S RESPONSIBILITIES

The seller's primary responsibility after closing is to vacate the property and ensure it is in the agreed-upon condition. This often involves a final clean-up and removal of all personal belongings. The seller should also make any agreed-upon repairs or improvements. It's important for the seller to leave the property in a clean and habitable state, not only as a matter of courtesy but also because it may be stipulated in the purchase agreement.

Moreover, the seller should ensure that all keys, remote controls for garage doors or gates, and any necessary codes or passwords are handed over to the buyer. If there are any warranties or manuals for appliances or systems left in the house, the seller should leave them for the buyer.

BUYER'S RESPONSIBILITIES

On the other hand, the buyer has several tasks to complete after the closing. One of the first tasks is to arrange for utilities to be transferred into their name. This includes electricity, water, gas, and other services like internet and cable. It's crucial to coordinate the timing of this transfer to avoid any disruption in services.

The buyer should also update their address with relevant entities such as banks, credit card companies, insurance providers, and the postal service. This ensures that all important documents and correspondences reach the correct address.

Another important post-closing responsibility for the buyer is to properly store and file all closing documents. These documents are important for tax purposes and for any future sale of the property. They serve as a legal proof of ownership and may be required by lenders or real estate agents in the future.

MUTUAL RESPONSIBILITIES

Both parties should keep copies of all closing documents for their records. These documents contain important information and may be needed in the future for tax purposes, refinancing, or resolving any potential disputes. It's a good idea to keep these documents in a safe place and to have them digitally scanned and stored as well.

In summary, the closing of a real estate transaction is not the end of responsibilities for the buyer and the seller. Both parties have important tasks to complete after the closing to ensure a smooth transition and to protect their respective interests. By understanding and fulfilling these post-closing responsibilities, both parties can help ensure a successful conclusion to the real estate transaction.

PROPERTY INSPECTION AND APPRAISAL

IN THE REALM OF REAL estate transactions, two critical steps that precede the finalization of any sale are the property inspection and the appraisal. These processes serve as protective measures for both the buyer and the lender involved in the transaction.

PROPERTY INSPECTION

The property inspection is typically initiated by the buyer and involves a thorough examination of the property by a professional inspector. The goal of this inspection is to uncover any potential issues that might not be immediately apparent, such as structural problems, plumbing or electrical issues, or potential health hazards like mold or asbestos.

The inspector provides a detailed report outlining any discovered issues, which the buyer can then use to negotiate repairs or a lower price with the seller. In some cases, severe issues may even lead the buyer to reconsider the purchase altogether.

APPRAISAL

While the property inspection is primarily for the buyer's benefit, the appraisal is a requirement of the lender. The appraisal process involves a professional appraiser determining the market value of the property based on various factors such as its condition, location, and comparison with similar properties recently sold in the area. The appraisal serves to protect the lender by ensuring that the loan amount does not exceed the property's worth. If the appraisal comes in lower than the agreed-upon sale price, it can lead to a renegotiation of the offer, or in some cases, the buyer may need to make up the difference.

THE IMPACT OF INSPECTION AND APPRAISAL RESULTS

The results of the property inspection and appraisal can significantly impact the trajectory of a real estate transaction. Discrepancies or issues discovered during these processes can lead to negotiations between the buyer and seller. For instance, the buyer may request that the seller address certain issues before closing, or they may ask for a reduction in the purchase price to account for the cost of repairs.

In some cases, if the issues are too significant or if the appraisal comes in much lower than the sale price, it could lead to the reevaluation or even cancellation of the offer. Therefore, these processes are crucial in ensuring a fair and transparent real estate transaction.

In the end, the property inspection and appraisal are not just procedural steps in a real estate transaction. They are vital tools that protect the interests of the buyer and the lender, helping to ensure that the property in question is a sound investment. By understanding the importance of these processes, all parties involved can navigate the complexities of real estate transactions with confidence and peace of mind.

CONTINGENCIES AND NEGOTIATIONS IN REAL ESTATE TRANSACTIONS

Contingencies and negotiations play a pivotal role in ensuring a smooth transaction. They serve as safety nets for both buyers and sellers, allowing them to navigate the complexities of the process with confidence.

UNDERSTANDING CONTINGENCIES

Contingencies are conditions or actions that must be met for a real estate contract to become binding. They are typically included in a buyer's offer to purchase a property and provide a legal means for the buyer to back out of the agreement without penalty if certain conditions are not met.

One common contingency is the financing contingency. This stipulates that the sale is dependent on the buyer securing adequate financing from a bank or other lending institution. If the buyer is unable to secure financing and has included a financing contingency in their offer, they can withdraw from the contract without losing their earnest money deposit.

Another common contingency is the home sale contingency. This allows the buyer to back out of the contract if they are unable to sell their current home within a certain timeframe. This contingency is particularly useful for buyers who need the proceeds from their current home to finance the purchase of a new one.

THE ROLE OF NEGOTIATIONS

Once a buyer makes an offer with contingencies, it is up to the seller to decide whether to accept the offer, reject it, or negotiate the terms. Negotiations in real estate transactions can cover a wide range of issues, including the price, closing date, and contingencies.

For instance, if a seller is eager to close quickly, they might negotiate to shorten the timeframe for the buyer's financing or home sale contingency. Alternatively, if the buyer's offer is significantly below the asking price, the seller might agree to a lower price but insist on removing the contingencies.

Negotiations can also occur after the home inspection. If the inspection reveals issues with the property, the buyer can request that the seller make repairs or provide a credit at closing to cover the cost of the repairs. The seller can agree to these terms, offer a counterproposal, or decline the request, which could prompt further negotiation.

STRIKING A BALANCE

The negotiation process requires both parties to strike a balance between protecting their interests and working towards a mutually beneficial outcome. While buyers want to ensure they are making a sound investment, sellers aim to maximize their return. Contingencies provide a structured way for these diverse interests to be addressed and negotiated.

In the end, the goal of both contingencies and negotiations is to ensure that both the buyer and seller feel confident and satisfied with the transaction. By understanding and effectively navigating these aspects, individuals can make informed decisions that align with their real estate goals. Every real estate transaction is unique, and the terms, conditions, and negotiations will vary based on the specific circumstances of the buyer and seller. Therefore, it is always advisable to engage the services of a knowledgeable real estate professional who can provide guidance throughout the process. Their expertise can prove invaluable in navigating the complexities of contingencies and negotiations in real estate transactions.

CLOSING AND TRANSFER OF OWNERSHIP

The process of closing and transferring ownership is a critical stage in the real estate transaction. It is the culmination of weeks, sometimes months, of hard work, negotiation, and preparation. This is the point where the buyer finally takes legal possession of the property, and the seller receives the agreed-upon payment.

The closing date, often referred to as the settlement date, is typically set during the negotiation phase and is usually several weeks after the seller accepts the buyer's offer. On this day, all involved parties convene to finalize the transaction. This meeting can take place at a neutral location such as the office of a real estate attorney or agent, or virtually in some cases.

The buyer, seller, and their respective legal representatives are usually present at the closing. In some instances, a representative from the lending institution may also attend. The purpose of this meeting is to ensure that all necessary documents are signed and all funds are correctly distributed.

Before the closing date, the buyer should have completed all due diligence, including property inspections and securing financing. The buyer is also responsible for purchasing homeowner's insurance and providing proof of insurance to the lender.

At the closing, the buyer will pay the remaining balance of the purchase price. This payment typically includes the down payment and any costs not covered by the mortgage loan. The funds can be transferred in several ways, including cashier's check, wire transfer, or electronic funds transfer.

Once the funds have been received, the seller will sign the deed over to the buyer, officially transferring ownership rights. This deed includes the legal description of the property and the names of the old and new owners.

The keys are then handed over to the buyer. It is customary for the seller to vacate the property by the closing date, leaving it in the condition agreed upon in the contract. However, in some cases, the seller may be allowed to remain on the property for a period after the closing, as stipulated in a rent-back agreement.

After the closing, the transaction is recorded in the local land records office. This public record helps establish the buyer as the new legal owner and protects their ownership rights. The recording process can vary by location but generally involves submitting the signed deed and paying a recording fee.

The closing and transfer of ownership mark the end of the home buying process. However, for the new homeowner, it's just the beginning of their journey. They can now move into their new home and start making it their own. While this process is generally standard, it can vary depending on local laws and customs. Therefore, it's always recommended to consult with a real estate professional or attorney to understand the specifics of your situation.

CHAPTER 5:

THE BENEFITS OF A GOOD HOME INSPECTION

When you make the decision to sell your home, one of the first and most critical steps you must take is to arrange for inspections. This is a step that is often misunderstood and underestimated in its importance. Despite common misconceptions, conducting thorough and high-quality home inspections is not just a formality, but an essential part of the selling process.

The idea of a home inspection may seem daunting to some sellers. There may be a fear of uncovering potential issues that could negatively impact the sale. However, it is important to understand that attempting to conceal or overlook potential defects, in the hope that buyers won't discover them, is a flawed strategy. This approach can lead to a multitude of problems down the line, including potential legal issues.

In the real estate business, transparency is key. It is always better to address issues head-on rather than hoping they will go unnoticed. By conducting a thorough home inspection, sellers can identify any potential problems and address them before listing the property. This not only helps to ensure a smoother selling process but also helps to build trust with potential buyers.

Moreover, it is important to note that even if buyers do not include contingencies in their offers, most will still conduct a property inspection. This is a standard part of the buying process and is likely to uncover any issues that may have been overlooked. Therefore, it is in the seller's best interest to conduct their own inspection beforehand to prevent any surprises.

In addition, a thorough home inspection can also provide sellers with a better understanding of the value of their property. By identifying and addressing any potential issues, sellers can ensure they are pricing their property accurately. This can help to attract more potential buyers and ultimately lead to a successful sale.

Furthermore, home inspections are not just beneficial for sellers, but also for buyers. For buyers, a home inspection provides an assurance of the condition of the property. It allows them to make an informed decision and feel confident in their investment.

In real estate, knowledge is power. A thorough home inspection provides both sellers and buyers with the knowledge they need to navigate the selling and buying process with confidence. It ensures transparency, builds trust, and ultimately leads to successful real estate transactions. Therefore, the importance of home inspections in the real estate business cannot be overstated. It is a crucial step in the selling process that ensures a smooth and successful transaction for all parties involved.

The following are some reason why investing in quality inspections can help you secure a higher price for your home:

1. Enhanced Transparency

Transparency in real estate transactions is not just a desirable trait; it's a necessity. It forms the bedrock of trust between the buyer and the seller, and can significantly influence the outcome of a transaction. By providing a comprehensive disclosures package and being open about any defects, a seller positions themselves as trustworthy. This honesty is particularly appealing to buyers who are seeking a fair and transparent seller.

The importance of transparency begins with the disclosure package. A complete disclosures package is a comprehensive collection of documents that provides detailed information about the property. It typically includes items such as the property's title report, pest inspection report, natural hazard disclosure report, and other relevant documents. By providing this package, the seller demonstrates their commitment to transparency and sets the stage for a smooth transaction.

However, the disclosures package is just the beginning. The seller must also be transparent about any defects in the property. This includes not only obvious issues but also potential problems that may not be immediately apparent. By being upfront about these issues, the seller helps the buyer make an informed decision. This can prevent disputes down the line and contribute to a smoother transaction.

This level of transparency and honesty is particularly appealing to buyers. In a market where information is often asymmetric, buyers appreciate sellers who are open and honest. This not only helps them make better decisions but also builds trust. Trust, in turn, can facilitate negotiations and make the transaction process smoother.

However, it's important to note that not all buyers will react the same way to this transparency. Some buyers may choose to walk away from a property if they perceive that the seller has not conducted proper inspections or if the disclosed defects are too significant. This is a risk that comes with transparency, but it's a risk worth taking. After all, it's better to lose a buyer at the beginning of the process than to face disputes and legal issues after the transaction has been completed.

In the end, enhanced transparency is not just about providing a disclosures package or being honest about defects. It's about establishing trust, facilitating negotiations, and ensuring a smooth transaction. It's about showing buyers that you, as a seller, are committed to fairness and honesty. And in a market where trust is often hard to come by, this can make all the difference.

So, while some buyers may walk away, those who stay are likely to be more committed, more cooperative, and more satisfied with the transaction. And in the world of real estate, where referrals and reputation are everything, this can lead to more opportunities and success in the future.

Therefore, enhanced transparency is not just a strategy; it's a philosophy. It's a commitment to honesty, fairness, and respect for the buyer. And in the long run, it's a commitment that pays off. For by being transparent, you not only facilitate the current transaction but also lay the foundation for future success in the real estate business.

Remember, in real estate, as in life, honesty is always the best policy. And when it comes to selling properties, enhanced transparency is the best way to demonstrate that honesty. It's the key to building trust, facilitating transactions, and ultimately, achieving success in the real estate business.

2. Increased Chance of Non-Contingent Offers

IN THE REALM OF REAL estate transactions, the concept of non-contingent offers has been gaining traction. This trend is largely driven by the trust that buyers place in the thoroughness and transparency of the seller's inspection reports. When buyers perceive these reports as comprehensive and honest, they may be enticed to waive the property condition contingency.

The property condition contingency is a common clause in real estate contracts that allows the buyer to back out of the agreement if significant issues are discovered during the property inspection. This contingency serves as a safety net for buyers, protecting them from unforeseen problems that could potentially cost thousands of dollars to rectify.

However, when buyers waive this contingency, they essentially agree to purchase the property "as is," regardless of any issues that may be uncovered later. This waiver is a strong signal of the buyer's commitment to the transaction, and it eliminates a crucial negotiating point that buyers often use to lower the purchase price or request repairs.

By waiving the property condition contingency, buyers significantly increase the chances of closing escrow at the agreed-upon price. This is a major advantage for sellers, as it provides them with more certainty about the outcome of the transaction. Sellers can be confident that the deal will not fall through due to negotiation disputes over property conditions discovered during the inspection.

Moreover, non-contingent offers can make a buyer's offer more attractive in a competitive market. In situations where multiple offers are being considered, sellers may prefer a non-contingent offer, even if it is not the highest. The certainty of a smooth transaction can sometimes outweigh the allure of a higher price.

However, it's important to note that while non-contingent offers can benefit both buyers and sellers, they also carry risks. Buyers who waive the property condition contingency must be prepared to take on any necessary repairs or renovations themselves. They should have a thorough understanding of the property's condition before making this decision.

For sellers, providing thorough and transparent inspection reports is crucial in fostering the trust necessary for buyers to consider waiving the property condition contingency. Sellers should ensure that their inspection reports accurately represent the condition of the property to avoid potential legal disputes down the line.

In the end, the increased chance of non-contingent offers is a testament to the power of trust and transparency in real estate transactions. When buyers trust in the accuracy of the seller's inspection reports, they are more likely to waive contingencies, leading to smoother transactions and increased chances of closing escrow at the agreed-upon price. This trend underscores the importance of honesty and thoroughness in property inspections, and it highlights the evolving dynamics of negotiation in real estate transactions.

As we delve deeper into the intricacies of real estate business, it becomes evident that the landscape is continually shifting, with new trends and strategies emerging. The rise of non-contingent offers is just one example of these changes, and it offers valuable insights for both buyers and sellers navigating the market.

3. Reduced Negotiations During Escrow

In the world of real estate, the escrow period is a critical phase in the buying and selling process. It's a time when buyers have the opportunity to conduct their due diligence, inspecting the property for any potential issues that might affect the value or livability of the home. Any problems discovered during this period can become points of negotiation, potentially leading to a reduction in the selling price or requests for repairs.

One strategy that sellers can employ to reduce the likelihood of such negotiations is to conduct thorough inspections upfront. By identifying and disclosing any issues before the buyer's inspection, sellers can maintain greater control over the negotiation process.

Take, for instance, the example of a leaky roof. If a seller's inspection reveals this issue, it can be disclosed to potential buyers from the outset. This transparency accomplishes two key things. First, it establishes trust between the buyer and seller, as the seller is demonstrating honesty and integrity by revealing the problem rather than waiting for the buyer to discover it. Second, it makes it more difficult for the buyer to use the issue as a negotiation point to lower the price, as they were made aware of it before making their offer.

This strategy is not just about maintaining control over the negotiation process, but also about managing expectations. By disclosing issues upfront, sellers can set realistic expectations about the condition of the property. This can help to prevent surprises during the escrow period, which can often lead to deals falling through or delays in closing.

Moreover, conducting thorough inspections upfront can also provide sellers with the opportunity to address any major issues before listing the property. This can enhance the home's appeal to potential buyers and may even increase its market value. For example, fixing a leaky roof not only removes a potential negotiation point, but it also adds value to the home by ensuring it is in good repair.

It's important to note that while this strategy can reduce the likelihood of negotiations during escrow, it does not eliminate it entirely. Buyers may still find issues during their inspection that were not discovered during the seller's inspection. However, by being proactive and transparent, sellers can significantly reduce the chances of these issues becoming major sticking points.

In the end, the goal of any seller should be to facilitate a smooth and successful transaction. Reducing negotiations during escrow through upfront inspections is one strategy that can help achieve this goal. It fosters transparency, builds trust, and ultimately leads to a more positive experience for all parties involved.

4. Minimized Surprises During Escrow

The escrow process is a critical phase in any real estate transaction. It serves as a neutral ground where the interests of all parties involved - the buyer, the seller, and the lender - are protected. However, it is also during this period that major issues can surface, potentially derailing deals and causing significant delays.

One of the most effective ways to prevent such setbacks is to uncover potential issues as early as possible. This proactive approach not only minimizes surprises during escrow but also provides several other benefits.

Early Discovery of Major Issues

Discovering major issues early in the process is beneficial for several reasons. First, it allows sellers to address these issues before they become deal-breakers. Whether it's a structural problem with the property, a title dispute, or an issue with the financing, early detection gives sellers the opportunity to rectify the problem or adjust their expectations accordingly.

Second, early discovery of issues is crucial because they must be disclosed to subsequent buyers. Transparency is key in real estate transactions, and sellers are legally obligated to disclose known issues to potential buyers.

By identifying these issues early, sellers can provide full disclosure, thus fostering trust and confidence among prospective buyers.

ADJUSTING PRICING AND MARKETING STRATEGIES

Knowing about major issues early also allows sellers to adjust their pricing and marketing strategies. If a property has significant issues that will require costly repairs, sellers might need to lower their asking price to make the deal more appealing. Alternatively, they might choose to invest in fixing the issues to maintain their desired price point.

In terms of marketing, sellers can tailor their strategies based on the property's condition. For instance, if a property needs some work but is located in a desirable neighborhood, the marketing strategy might focus on the property's potential and the value of its location.

SMOOTH TRANSACTIONS AND SATISFIED PARTIES

Ultimately, the goal of minimizing surprises during escrow is to ensure smooth and successful real estate transactions. When major issues are discovered and addressed early, transactions are less likely to fall through, and all parties are more likely to be satisfied with the outcome.

By adopting a proactive approach, sellers can navigate the escrow process with confidence, secure in the knowledge that they have done everything possible to minimize surprises and ensure a successful sale. This not only leads to successful transactions but also contributes to a more transparent and trustworthy real estate industry.

5. Less Need for Additional Buyer Inspections

IN THE REAL ESTATE INDUSTRY, inspections play a crucial role in ensuring the quality and safety of a property. They provide an unbiased evaluation of a home's condition, giving both buyers and sellers a clear understanding of any potential issues that may need to be addressed. However, when inspections are conducted by reputable inspectors, there may be less need for additional buyer inspections. This can streamline the closing process and eliminate potential hurdles, offering several benefits.

TRUST IN PROFESSIONAL EXPERTISE

Reputable inspectors are professionals who have extensive training and experience in evaluating properties. They adhere to a strict code of ethics and standards of practice, ensuring that their inspections are thorough and accurate. When buyers trust in this professional expertise, they may feel confident accepting the inspection report and forgoing additional inspections. This trust can save time and resources, as buyers do not need to seek out and coordinate with another inspector.

STREAMLINING THE CLOSING PROCESS

The closing process in real estate transactions can be complex and time-consuming. It involves numerous steps, from securing financing and title insurance to conducting inspections and appraisals. By accepting the initial inspection report and forgoing additional inspections, buyers can streamline this process. They can move forward more quickly with negotiations, loan approval, and other closing tasks. This can lead to a smoother, more efficient transaction, benefiting all parties involved.

ELIMINATING POTENTIAL HURDLES

Additional inspections can introduce potential hurdles to the closing process. They may reveal new issues that need to be addressed, leading to further negotiations or even causing the deal to fall through. By accepting the initial inspection report, buyers can eliminate these potential hurdles. They can proceed with the transaction with a clear understanding of the property's condition, reducing the risk of unexpected surprises that could derail the closing process.

MAINTAINING MOMENTUM IN THE TRANSACTION

Real estate transactions often involve a certain momentum. Once an offer is accepted, the buyer and seller typically want to move forward as quickly as possible to close the deal. Additional inspections can slow down this momentum, introducing delays and potentially causing frustration. By forgoing additional inspections, buyers can maintain the momentum of the transaction, keeping the process moving forward smoothly and efficiently.

In summary, when inspections are conducted by reputable inspectors, there may be less need for additional buyer inspections. This can offer several benefits, from streamlining the closing process to eliminating potential hurdles and maintaining momentum in the transaction. It underscores the importance of hiring a reputable inspector and trusting in their professional expertise. By doing so, buyers can feel confident in their understanding of the property's condition and proceed with the transaction in a more efficient and effective manner. This approach can contribute to a smoother, more successful real estate transaction, benefiting both buyers and sellers alike.

6.. Opportunity for Pre-Market Fixes

THE REAL ESTATE MARKET IS a dynamic environment where trust and value play pivotal roles. One of the most effective ways to build trust with potential buyers and add value to a property is by addressing any issues before listing it on the market. This process, known as pre-market fixing, can significantly enhance the appeal of a property, potentially leading to higher prices and increased interest from buyers.

Pre-market fixes can range from minor cosmetic updates to major structural repairs. Regardless of the extent, these improvements signal to buyers that the seller is proactive and has taken steps to ensure the property is in the best possible condition. This not only builds trust but also saves buyers time as they can focus on the property's features rather than potential problems.

When sellers take the initiative to make these improvements, they demonstrate a level of transparency that buyers appreciate. It shows that the seller is not trying to hide any potential issues, which can often be a concern for buyers. This transparency can lead to a smoother transaction process, as there are fewer surprises that could delay or derail negotiations.

Moreover, pre-market fixes can also increase the perceived value of the property. A well-maintained property is more likely to attract buyers and command a higher price. Buyers are often willing to pay a premium for properties that are move-in ready and require little to no immediate work. By addressing issues upfront, sellers can position their property as a desirable, hassle-free option for buyers.

Additionally, pre-market fixes can help differentiate a property in a competitive market. With so many properties available, buyers can afford to be selective. A property that has been well cared for and prepared for sale can stand out from the crowd, attracting more interest and, ultimately, more offers.

Furthermore, by dealing with any issues before listing, sellers can avoid the risk of a potential buyer discovering a problem during the home inspection that could lead to renegotiations or even the cancellation of the sale. This proactive approach can help ensure a faster, smoother sale process, benefiting both the seller and the buyer.

While pre-market fixes require an investment of time and money, the potential benefits can far outweigh the costs. Higher sale prices, increased buyer interest, and a smoother transaction process are just a few of the advantages that make pre-market fixes a worthwhile consideration for sellers.

To wrap up, pre-market fixes present a valuable opportunity for sellers in the real estate market. By addressing issues before listing, sellers can build trust with buyers, enhance the appeal of their property, and potentially achieve a higher sale price. This proactive approach not only benefits the seller but also creates a more positive and efficient experience for the buyer, contributing to a successful real estate transaction.

Your realtor can recommend reliable service providers for inspections. It is advisable to choose thorough inspectors who prioritize disclosure. A home inspection and pest inspection are essential, and other inspections can be ordered as needed.

I believe in the importance of comprehensive inspections. That's why I recommend service providers who prioritize thoroughness and disclosure. If you have any questions or would like to discuss inspections further, feel free to schedule a meeting. Your realtor can assist you with the process.

REFERENCES AND BIBLIOGRAPHY

Ferry, Mike. The Mike Ferry Sales System. YouTube playlist. Accessed February 27, 2024. youtu.be/playlist?list=PLOnHmRn9Gtz6hmaEzlewg_4QXXw9uVS2P

Engmann, Sean. "6 Reasons Inspections Will Help You Get a Higher Price for Your Home." YouTube video. Accessed February 27, 2024. youtu.be/wmG3Mn7SMlw?si=zblUfYpvVCUkFzoJ

ExpertRealEstateTips. YouTube channel. Accessed February 27, 2024. youtu.be/@ExpertRealEstateTips/playlist

Kehr, Ashley. The Real Estate Rookie. Denver, CO: BiggerPockets Publishing LLC, 2023.

Turner, Brandon. The Book on Rental Property Investing. BiggerPockets Publishing LLC, 2015.

Tyson, Eric, and Robert S. Griswold. Real Estate Investing for Dummies. John Wiley & Sons; 3rd edition (February 23, 2015)

Martinez, Matthew A. Investing in Apartment Buildings. McGraw Hill; 1st edition (November 11, 2008)

ABOUT THE AUTHOR

KAREN VERSACE HAS BEEN RECOGNIZED as one the top agents in the United States and she also considers herself as her client's concerned friend that will go hand and hand with them in every step of the way. She grew her business by word of mouth and referrals from her happy and satisfied past clients that needed to sell or buy their home or other investment properties. She has done a phenomenal job in all her Real Estate transactions including short sales. Her main goal is to understand exactly what every client needs and wants and execute them thoroughly. For her, the key to a successful Real Estate transaction is making sure everybody is in good communication and she always manages to do things in favor on her client's best interest.

Karen Versace

Realtor
NAR, LRES, Short Sale Specialist

Direct:
(310) 880-4353

Office:
(626) 820-1920

License:
01766651

Email:
realtorkarenversace@gmail.com